D1741236

7 Master Secrets

to
Becoming a
Distinguished University
or
College Student

by
Bheki Shabangu

authorHOUSE®

AuthorHouse™ UK Ltd.
500 Avebury Boulevard
Central Milton Keynes, MK9 2BE
www.authorhouse.co.uk
Phone: 08001974150

First published by AuthorHouse 2/17/2009

ISBN: 978-1-4389-3644-4 (sc)

Printed in the United States of America
Bloomington, Indiana

This book is printed on acid-free paper.

Contents

Acknowledgements

The content of this book is the product of the investment various people have made in my life. I am so grateful for Dr Myles Munroe and Dr Mike Murdock. Dr Mike Murdock has had a tremendous impact on my life and has been the key inspiration to write this book. He challenged me to start documenting my persuasions. I thank him so much. Also, thanks go to Sarah-Jane Attard, my protégé, for being an inspiration in pursuit of her actress, dance, and choreography career. And finally, I thank my beautiful mother, Thembekile, for being the one to introduce me to this world. Mama, your gentleness and kindness are extra-ordinary.

Bheki Shabangu

Foreword

Some students don't really know what they want out of university or college; they drift through classes, performing adequately (or badly) on exams, and eventually get some sort of job after graduation that they probably could have got even without their degrees. These are the un-distinguished college or university students. Other students really stand out. They know what they want in life, and they organise themselves and their studies to make sure they get it. Bheki Shabangu – who was once a most distinguished student and is now a successful professional – has some excellent advice on how to be this sort of student. His seven "Master Secrets" are powerful tools for making sure you stand out among your fellow students and are best positioned to make the most of your education. Also, when you are ready to enter the world, this advice will continue to be useful – because the most distinguished people never stop being students of some sort; they never stop learning. Bheki Shabangu gives advice for distinguished learning and distinguished living. Use it well!

Dr Pegram Harrison, Director, Emerging Leaders Programme, London Business School

Introduction

In 1990, a group of Christians climbed to the top of a mountain in New Zealand, vowing on national television that they weren't coming down until Christ returned. I am sure that they have all returned back to their jobs and families if not sacked. I doubt if these were people of vision. Visionaries are focused. They are not time wasters. Every moment counts to them. They always have something to accomplish. Vision provides motivation. Find me a man or woman who lacks motivation, and I'll show you someone with little or no vision. A life without vision or purpose is a life of frustrations. Vision or purpose helps you to live a distinguished life. A distinguished life is not an accident. It requires diligence. A distinguished life will cost you time, energy, and focus. Success in life goes to the person who has the courage to dream, the ability to organise, and the strength to execute. Becoming a distinguished person is possible. History is filled with inspiring stories of people who fought against the odds and succeeded. What is your attitude towards success or living a distinguished life? A study by Harvard University found that when people get jobs, 85 per cent of the time, it is because of their attitude. Only 15 per cent of the time it is because of how smart they are and how many facts and figures they know. Your attitude will always be a determinant of your level of achievement or success. *The sky is not the limit.* All things are possible. Only you can determine the degree or level of your success. Many resent success, but envy the successful. You were born to live a distinguished life. When God made you, he immediately threw a formula. In that equation of a formula, is a variable which represents a distinguished life. The amount to which you adjust this variable will determine the amplitude or height of the level of your success. You are responsible for your success. The degree of your success will be determined by your decisions, your willingness, and your determination to succeed. Success will always distinguish you from the crowds. I want you to know that you are already on your way to living a life of significance. The fact that you are holding this book in your hands is a photograph of your journey to becoming a distinguished university or college student.

1

Clearly Defined Vision

When your heart decides the destination, your mind will design the map to reach it.

Dr Mike Murdock

Capital isn't scarce; vision is.

Sam Walton

Where there is no vision, the people perish.

Proverbs

Helen Keller, who was born blind and deaf, said, "The greatest tragedy to befall a person is to have sight but lack vision". What is a vision? A vision is a preferred future. It is a clear mental picture of what could be. An effective vision has four vital components:

❶ The problem

❷ The solution to the problem

❸ The reason something should be done

❹ The reason something must be done now

What is your vision? What do you see yourself doing in the future? What is the problem your vision will address? The problem is not the vision. The solution is the vision. The problem provides a clear context for presenting the vision. As a university or college student, I urge you to dream big. Begin to elevate the picture of your future. You can't think of catching mice and expect to catch lions. Vision is of paramount importance. It translates into purpose. A vision gives you a reason to get up in the morning. A lack of vision is the reason many never finish what they start. Vision provides motivation.

Your vision is your future. A person without a vision is a person without a future. A person without a future will always go back to his or her past. Therefore, it is critical that you develop a clear and succinct vision for your life. Why do you exist? Your vision should be written down. When you write it down, it forces you to clarify it. Bear in mind that your vision will attract critics. Never hand it over to their hands. Visions often die at the hands of the critics. Critics are spectators, not players. Critical people are disappointed people. Remember, there has never been a monument built to a critic. A man called Nehemiah in the bible noticed that the walls needed to be rebuilt. He decided to take responsibility in rebuilding the walls. As he started to make progress, critics began to throw stones at him and sending intimidating letters to stop him. They slandered and undermined his work. Some even said that if a fox walked on the walls, they would collapse. What did he do? He simply disregarded their voices. I am fascinated by his response. Nehemiah said, "I am doing a great work and I cannot come down".

Critics want you to come down to their level. They feel intimidated by your vision. Anyone unhappy over your success or progress is your enemy. Swiftly disconnect yourself before these people poison you. In all their attempts to frustrate your progress, they will fail. A man or woman of vision is unstoppable.

Visionaries understand that what is inside them is greater than everything else around them. I dare you to dream big! If you can imagine it, you can achieve it. If you can dream it, you can become it. A dynamic life is always fired by a vision. *A clearly defined vision is one of the master secrets to becoming a distinguished university or college student.*

Fundamentals

❶ A vision is a preferred future.

❷ A vision is a mental picture of your future.

❸ Your vision is your future.

❹ Your vision should be written down.

❺ Your vision will attract critics.

❻ A man or woman of vision is unstoppable.

❼ A dynamic life is always fired by a vision.

2

Goals-Setting

A goal properly set is halfway reached.

Abraham Lincoln

Crystallize your goals. Make a plan for achieving them and set yourself a deadline. Then, with supreme confidence, determination, and disregard for obstacles and other people's criticism, carry out your plan.

Paul Meyer

Albert Schweitzer once said that, "the tragedy of life is not that we die, but what dies inside a man while he lives". Many people walk around with feelings of dissatisfaction and defeat because of dead dreams and visions that once lit the fires in their hearts. It is not over until you win! You can begin right now to rekindle those dreams and vision. A life of pleasure and fulfilment is possible.

What are goals? Webster's dictionary defines a goal as "the end toward which effort is directed, to forecast for one's future". A goal is not a plan. A plan is a written list of arranged actions necessary to achieve your desired goals. Goals are vision with feet. They are a set of specific, measurable steps to achieve the vision. The establishment of goals is the way to fulfil your vision. Your vision must remain permanent, but your goals must remain flexible. A goal without a deadline is a wish. Without setting goals, your vision and dreams are just wishful thinking. Goal-setting is a habit of great achievers.

In 1952, a prominent university discovered that only three out of a hundred graduates had written down a clear list of their goals. In years later, their follow-up study showed that 3 per cent of the graduating class had accomplished more financially than the remaining 97 per cent of the class. Those 3 per cent were the same graduates who had written down their goals. When you write down your goal, statisticians say, you increase your chance of obtaining it by 90 per cent. I would advice that you involve others in your goals. Relationship skills will be necessary for you to achieve your goals.

It is said that only 3 per cent of the people on earth have their goals written down. Bob Richards, a pole vault gold medallist said, "You hit no higher than you aim". The higher you aim, the further you will go. The quality of your goals will determine the quality of your success. Your goals are the only exit from your zone of frustration and dissatisfaction into the zone of fulfilment and happiness. Goals separate achievers from dreamers. Paul J. Meyer, who is regarded as the founder of personal development said, "75 per cent of his personal success has come as a result of goal-setting. The remaining 25 per cent would be a combination of focus, desire, preparation, and hard work".

Goal-setting is very powerful. It takes your dreams and turns them into reality. When setting goals, there are four different kinds to include in your plan:

❶ Short-range goals (6 months or less)

❷ Long-range goals (1 year to a lifetime)

❸ Tangible goals (These have to do with needs and wants e.g. increasing your income)

❹ Intangible goals (These are personal goals that affect your character. They are the basis for your tangible goals. They include spiritual, mental, emotional goals, and so forth)

The process of goal-setting helps you to choose the direction of your life. Your goals must be **SMART**.

- **S** – Specific
- **M** – Measurable
- **A** – Attainable
- **R** – Realistic
- **T** – Time-bound

◈ **Specific**

Your goals must be straightforward and emphasize what you want to happen. Clarity helps to focus your efforts. Specific means asking yourself what are you going to do? Why is it important to do this at this time? How are you going to do it?

◈ Measurable

Your goals have to be measurable so that you can monitor your progress. If not measurable, how will you see when you reach your goals? Consider this example: "I want to read a seven-chapter book of one hundred pages from January to February." This shows the specific target to be measured. "I want to be a good reader" is not as measurable.

◈ Attainable

Goals that are too far out of your reach are difficult to commit to. As an example, if you aim to lose 20 lbs in one week, this is ridiculous and impossible! You can never achieve this within a week. But losing 1 lb is possible. When you have achieved that, aiming to loose a further 1 lb will keep it achievable for you.

◈ Realistic

Realistic is not synonymous with easy. Realistic means do-able. You must consider where you are before you navigate to where you want to be. Many people want to get somewhere, but they haven't the slightest clue of where they are.

◈ Time-bound

Put a time limit to your goal. We said that a goal without a deadline is a wish. Putting a time frame on your goal gives you a clear target to work towards. If you don't have a time frame, there will be no urgency to take action.

Remember that your goals will change as you get older. In reaching your goals, you will face obstacles. It is a fact of life. Your interpretation or perception of those obstacles is paramount. Do you see them as walls or as bridges to your next level? I want you to know that obstacles, when viewed properly, will only intensify your desire and multiply your energy. You will overcome them beyond any shadow of a doubt.

True achievers invest time and energy to develop clear-cut written goals. I urge you to write down everything you *want*, everything you would like to *become*, *do*, or *have* during your lifetime. You must decide what you want. When you decide exactly what you want, the plan of how to do it will emerge. Life is a journey. Every journey has a destination. Your goals are a flight that will take you to your desired and well-defined destination. You will reach your destination. *Goal-setting is one of the master secrets to becoming a distinguished university or college student.*

Fundamentals

❶ A goal is not a plan.

❷ A goal without a deadline is a wish.

❸ Goals are sets of specific, measurable steps to achieve the vision.

❹ When you write down your goal, you increase the chance of obtaining it by 90 per cent.

❺ The process of goal-setting helps you to choose the direction of your life.

❻ True achievers invest time and energy to develop clear-cut written goals.

❼ Your goals will change as you get older.

❽ Relationship skills are necessary for you to achieve your goals.

3

Passion and Focus

We may affirm that absolutely nothing great in the world has been accomplished without passion.

Georg Wilhelm Friedrich Hegel

Concentrate all your thoughts upon the work at hand. The sun's rays do not burn until brought to a focus.

Alexander Graham Bell

Henry Kaizer said, "Determine what you want more than anything else in life, write down the means by which you intend to attain it, and permit nothing to defer you from pursuing it". There are four kinds of people who always fail:

1. Those who are undecided
2. Those who are unlearned
3. Those who are unfocused
4. Those who are unexcited

If you want to achieve your dreams and vision, you have to be decisive, apply yourself, and stay focused. The reason many fail is because of the lack of focus. Decisiveness, passion, and focus are necessary for you to attain your dreams and vision.

When Henry Ford decided to produce his famous V-8 motor, he chose to build an engine with the entire eight-cylinder cast in one block. He instructed his engineers to produce a design for the engine. The design was placed on paper, but the engineers agreed that it was impossible to cast an eight-cylinder engine block in one piece. Ford said, "Produce it anyway". But they again replied that it was impossible. Ford commanded them to go ahead with the plan. He told them to stay on the job until they succeeded, no matter how much time was required. The engineers went ahead. There was nothing else for them to do if they were to remain on the Ford staff.

Six months went by; nothing happened. Another six months passed, and still nothing happened. The engineers tried every conceivable plan to carry out the orders, but it seemed impossible. At the end of the year, Ford checked with his engineers, and again they informed him they had found no way to carry out his orders. "Go right ahead", said Ford. "I want it, and I'll have it." They went ahead, and then, as if by a stroke of magic, the secret was discovered. Ford's unwavering decisiveness kept his engineers from giving up too early.

What is passion? Passion is not interest. Passion is an intense desire. The proof of your passion is pursuit. You have no right to anything you have not pursued. You can never have significant success without passion. Many people with great potential and great dreams have lost their passion to achieve them. The graveyards are filled with buried dreams, buried treasures, and buried possibilities that were never fulfilled. They failed to protect their passion. People who succeed greatly possess great passion.

Disciplined focus is what distinguishes those who make things happen from those who merely watch things happen. Eagles have been observed roosting for hours above a rabbit hole, a snake hole, or a place where fish or birds have disappeared. The raptor will wait and wait, sometimes for hours. Usually the bird's patience is rewarded. The prey will show its head, and, like lightning, the eagle strikes with devastating speed and power.

On your journey to attaining your dreams and vision, there will be people who will try to break your focus and weaken your passion. These people are wrong to do so. They do not belong in your life. Identify them, and swiftly move away from them.

Some people believe that their main purpose for existence is to hinder others from their progress or success. They will begin to hold negative opinions about you and start talking you down. Never allow yourself to become a slave to the opinions of others. Does an eagle ask a turkey how high it is allowed to fly? Never! You must develop a singleness of purpose for you to accomplish your dreams and vision. Passion and focus is the only difference between your success and failure. *The combination of passion and focus is one of the master secrets to becoming a distinguished university or college student.*

Fundamentals

❶ Passion is not interest. Passion is an intense desire.

❷ The proof of your passion is pursuit.

❸ You do not have a right to anything you have not pursued.

❹ You must develop a singleness of purpose for you to accomplish your dreams and vision.

❺ Lack of focus results to failure.

❻ Passion and focus are necessary for you to attain your vision.

4

Self-Portrait

As a man thinketh in his heart, so he is.

Proverbs

A story is told of a young boy who was six-foot-seven at thirteen years of age. He carried feelings of inadequacy in himself. He listened to the lies about himself, that he was no good, there was something wrong with him, and he would never amount to anything. One day his father said, "Son, are you coming to the prayer meeting tonight"? A young boy said, "No dad, I am going to stay home and study for my final exam". The young boy said to his father, "but will you please bring home a pizza after the prayer meeting?" And as his father came home with a hot pizza sitting on the front seat of his Mercedes Benz, he hit the electric garage door opener. The headlight of his car caught his son swinging from the rafter. He had hung himself. A young boy's friend was asked to tell the story. His friend said, "Satan so filled my friend with lies, that he hated himself. His mind was so filled with such lies that the only escape he could do was to make his final exit." The friend continued to say, "Satan took *my friends hands* and tied a rope around his neck and threw it over the rafter with *his hands*. He brought the chair and with *his feet* Satan stood him on top of it. And with *his other foot* he kicked the chair out from under it."

How sad could this be? You see, Satan couldn't have done it without his co-operation. None of the propaganda, none of the lies that have ever been perpetrated can affect you in any way, shape, or form, unless you believe it. And when you believe it, you become an accomplice of the very force that seeks to destroy you. An inferiority complex is the most hideous, insidious form of slavery.

Friend, the greatest battle ever waged did not take place in Rwanda or Vietnam. It did not take place during WWII, nor was it the invasion of Afghanistan or Iraq. The greatest battle ever to be fought will dwarf the battle of Armageddon by comparison. This battle is in progress right now, and it is being waged in the arena of your mind! I urge you to guard your sensory perceptions by taking care what you expose your eyes and ears to. Guard your perceptors. *Garbage in, garbage out!* What you take in will stay with you a long time, regardless of its quality. Never put anything in front of you that you do not want in your future. For example, be very selective in what you hear. Choose to listen to tapes or CDs that inspire you. You must learn to create an environment that inspires you. In a very interesting story from my favourite book, the Bible, twelve spies were sent by Moses, who had at last led the nation of Israel from slavery to the place that God had promised them as a nation. These twelve men were key leaders who represented every tribe of Israel. They came back and gave an account on what they had seen. Ten spies came back with a horrifying report. They said the place was indeed flowing with milk and honey;

nevertheless the place could not be easily penetrated, and the people who dwelt in the land were giants. They even brought back with them clusters of grapes to prove to the people that the place was exactly what God had promised them they would possess. The fearful meant went on to say, "We saw ourselves as grasshoppers in their own sight". It is interesting that the giants never said anything; this was their own conclusion.

Two spies out of the twelve came back with a different report. They said, "It is true that the people who dwell in the land are giants, nevertheless we are able to take the land". What was the difference between the ten and the two spies? The two spies had a good self-portrait. You see, what you focus on becomes magnified. The two spies chose to focus on the victory that lay ahead of their immediate challenge. They saw the spoils beyond the giants. In contrast, the ten spies focused on the giants. The two spies were confident in the fact that the one who had promised was able to give them victory over their enemies. The two spies had a right picture of themselves. The way you see yourself decides your conduct. You will always act like the person you think you are.

As a man thinketh, so he is. What do you think of yourself? Are you the result of an accident, a random occurrence? What effigy do you carry of yourself? *Friend, God makes no junk.* You are unique and special. You possess a unique set of fingerprints. There has never been you before. There are approximately more than 6.73 billion people on the earth today, and none of them has your set of fingerprints. You are one of a kind. You are not a copy but an original. You are irreplaceable. So get excited about yourself!

What is a self-portrait? A self-portrait is your mental picture of yourself. This picture is made up of what you believe about your talents and abilities, your worth as a person, how you expect others to accept you, what you believe you can become, and, finally, what you believe about how you came into existence. Why is it so important to have a good self-portrait? You can never rise above the picture you have of yourself. Your success will be determined by this picture.

This presents a challenge for many. Statistics tell us that 30 per cent of women and approximately 20 per cent of men have been sexually abused as children. Also, the vast majority of children come from single-parent families. Many suffered traumatic events leading to or following a divorce. They have never received closure from these events, and, as a result, their minds are taken hostage by harmful mindsets. I urge you to correct every wrong picture you have of yourself. Rebuild a good picture of yourself. Don't become a slave to your past. Do not allow your past to bleed into your future. Never allow past hurts and failures to imprison you in the jail of yesterday. You can't drive fast staring in the rear-view mirror.

A distorted picture of yourself can result in an inferiority complex. A grasshopper complex is a deadly disease. It will sabotage every dream within you. I want you to know that you can recover from any past traumatic experience. Recovery is possible.

Listen to this truth. A man does not drown by falling into the river; he drowns by staying there. I say recovery is possible! Rise up. Pick up every scattered piece of your life. Submit it to God. Out of your brokenness, He will make your life beautiful. From this day, begin to lift your shoulders high and start talking like a victor instead of a victim. You will never reach the palace talking like a peasant. The way you see yourself decides your conduct. Furthermore, how you see yourself will determine how others see you. And you will always permit the treatment you think you deserve. *A good self-portrait is one of the master secrets to becoming a distinguished university or college student.*

Fundamentals

❶ You can never rise above the picture you have of yourself.

❷ The way you see yourself decides your conduct.

❸ How you see yourself will determine how others see you.

❹ You will always act like the person you think you are.

❺ You will always permit the treatment you think you deserve.

❻ What you hear and see is deciding who you become.

5

Choice of Your Future Career

Trust not what inspires other members of society to choose a career. Trust what inspires you. From this decision alone will come over a third of your satisfaction or misery in your life.

> *The Lazy Person's Guide to Success*

You never stop earning when you do what you love.

> *Asha Tyson*

Choosing your vocation is one of the most important choices you will ever make in your life. Some choose their career paths based on what their friends want to do. Some are influenced by their families. This is your life. You live only once. You cannot afford to live on wrong choices. Never allow anyone to dictate what you pursue. Please do take advice, but always follow what you are passionate about because this is where you will succeed. What are the signposts to your future career path?

Here are few indicators that can assist you in making a good choice:

❶ What do you love to talk about?

❷ What do you love to think about?

❸ What do you love to learn about?

❹ Where do you invest most of your time?

❺ If every person were paid the same salary, what would you do?

These indicators clearly show what you love. What you love the most is the indication of the path you must pursue. Remember that you are not born qualified, you must become qualified. This means that you have to prepare yourself for your future career. The only difference between your success and failure is preparation. The quality of your preparation will always determine the quality of your performance: proper preparation results in proper performance; improper preparation results in improper performance. Great concert pianists invest hundreds of hours of practice before a concert. Champions do not become champions in the ring. They are merely recognised in the ring. They had to become champions beforehand. People stumble over pebbles instead of climbing the mountain because of lack of preparation. I can't stress enough the significance of preparation. Preparation time is never wasted time; however, please bear in mind that great efforts do not always produce immediate results.

I urge you to invest everything it takes to become the best in your area of expertise. Everything that is important is costly. To become the best, you must learn from the best. Build your library around your area of expertise. Invest in appropriate and relevant seminars. Stay current by reading journals and subscribing to magazines and other publications within the field of your choice.

I would advice that you find a mentor who is already doing what you want to do. If your area of interest is law or real estate, who do you know in your local area? You must schedule appointments with them. Pursue people who have been where you want to go. They have done something you want to accomplish. You must pursue those who are qualified, not those who are available.

Mentors are the key to your success. A mentor is not someone you listen to, but someone whose advice you follow. Clearly define your expectations from your mentors. How do you want them to help you? You must always remain teachable. Be sure to value and respect your mentor's discoveries. Where there is enough counsel or advice, dreams and vision are prone to succeed. Merely having advice is not the key to success: applying *good* advice is the key to extraordinary success. *The choice of the right career is one of the master secrets to becoming a distinguished university or college student.*

Fundamentals

❶ What you love the most is the indication of the career path you must pursue.

❷ You are not born qualified, you must become qualified.

❸ The only difference between success and failure is preparation.

❹ The quality of your preparation will always determine the quality of your performance.

❺ Great efforts do not always produce immediate results.

❻ To become the best, you must learn from the best.

❼ Pursue people who have been where you want to go.

❽ Mentors are the key to your success.

6

Choice of Your Future Mate

Don't marry the person you think you can live with; marry only the individual you think you can't live without.

Dr James C. Dobson

The greatest mistake you will ever make in life is to marry the wrong person. Your late discoveries after your commitment can destroy your entire life. Who is the wrong person? The wrong person is someone who does not admire your achievements. The wrong person is someone who is disrespectful of your goals and vision. Your speed of progress towards the fulfilment of your dreams and vision will be determined by the person you allow to have access to your life. The right person will energise you. The wrong person will exhaust you. The right person will become enthusiastic when you share your dreams and your goals with them.

Anyone who becomes unhappy over your success is your enemy. Whose voice have you been listening to? The person you trust is deciding your future. Your future mate has to be the one who will walk alongside you, supporting and encouraging you to fulfil your dreams and vision. Your future mate has to be the one who will protect your focus and create a climate of protection around you.

There are four kinds of people in your life. They are those who:
- ❶ Add
- ❷ Subtract
- ❸ Multiply
- ❹ Divide

For you to achieve your dreams and vision, those who add and multiply are necessary. They will multiply your passion and your focus. They will nurture your strengths instead of your weaknesses.

They will complement you in different areas of your life. Remember, that true love does not allow two people to compete with the success of one another.

What is true love anyway? Love cannot be measured. True love has no reason for existence. If anyone says, "I love you because of such-in-such reason", you're headed for serious danger! A reason becomes a condition. Where there's a condition, there's an expectation. Where there's an expectation, there's disappointment. Where there's disappointment, there's division. Where there's division, there's an end to the relationship. How did it start? It all started with a condition.

So, what is love? Love is a decision to commit to meeting the needs of another. Love is not a feeling. It is possible to have a thousand feelings about the same thing in one day. Therefore, love cannot be based on feelings. Feelings come and go; they are not stable. It would be unwise to build love on an unstable foundation. I urge you to start writing down the qualities of your ideal mate. I will use my list of qualities as an example. They are listed in order of their importance.

❶ Spirituality	-	Born-again Christian
❷ Character	-	Self-control (ability to control their behaviour no matter their emotions)
	-	Selflessness (desire to put another first)
	-	Accountability (ability to assume responsibility)
	-	Loyalty (faithfulness, dependability, integrity)
❸ Personality	-	Warm and friendly
	-	Enthusiastic
	-	Confident and bold
	-	Supportive
	-	Accommodating
	-	Extroverted
❹ Authenticity	-	Does not perform for life, but is genuine
❺ Appearance	-	Beautiful, approximately same height
❻ Ambitions	-	Common goals and interests regarding family and money
❼ Intelligence	-	"Wise as a serpent"
❽ Creativity	-	Productive and able to initiate

| ❾ Chemistry | - | Very, very strong |
| ❿ Parenting | - | Willing to learn (because parenting is a skill that doesn't come automatically) |

Please friend, don't even think about criticising my qualities. These are mine. Write yours. If you do not decide what you want, others will always decide for you. *Choosing the right future mate is one of the master secrets to becoming a distinguished university or college student.*

Fundamentals

❶ Your progress towards your dreams and vision will be determined by the person you allow to have access to your life.

❷ The person you trust is deciding your future.

❸ Anyone who becomes unhappy over your success is your enemy.

❹ True love does not compete with the success of another.

❺ Love is a decision to commit to meeting the needs of another.

7

Honouring Your Parents

Harken unto thy father that begat thee, and despise not thy mother when she is old.

Proverbs

Honour thy father and thy mother; that thy days may be long upon the land which the Lord thy God giveth thee.

Exodus

What does the word honour mean? Does it mean rolling on the floor in someone's presence? Does it imply kissing someone's feet? The word honour means to value, to show care and profound regard. A person you honour is someone you value and show respect to. Your father and your mother are vitally important in your life. They are the people who brought you here. If it were not for them, you wouldn't have existed. Have you taken the time to thank your parents for looking after you when you couldn't look after yourself? Those sleepless nights changing your diapers and feeding you weren't easy. By the way, I would like to remind you that you still owe your mother nine months of rent and food. I urge you to pay it as a form of gratitude. It has to be paid. Don't make excuses! Your parents provided you with shelter and put you through school. You might have not had the privilege of going to the best schools. At least they tried their best. Stop blaming your parents for what they could not deliver. Remember that when you blame another, you give up the power to change. Now you are here; you are responsible for charting the course of your own life. Your parents were the entry point through which you came into this world, but after that, you make your own choices.

Your relationship with your parents is of paramount importance to your future success. Have you taken time to rebuild the bridges of your relationship with your parents, no matter how much you have been hurt in the past? Maybe you have allowed resentment towards them to separate you from them. I urge you to go back and make things right. This is only for your benefit. Your future success hinges on your relationship with your parents. Honouring your parents has significant benefits. It will increase your length of days on this earth. Even the key to your financial future is honouring your parents. If you cannot honour or respect someone who clothed you, fed you, put you through school, and paid for your college or university, chances are slim that you will honour and respect the man or woman you marry in the future.

Now, what are some practical ways to show honour? Spend time with your parents. If you don't live near them, initiate a phone conversation. They long to hear from you. Please remember that your parents will not be around forever. Another practical way to show honour is to anticipate their needs, especially as they get older. You must be prepared to support them financially if necessary. It is your role and responsibility not to expose but to always cover their shame. Honouring parents is not something that is much talked about in our day and age, but it is crucial. It is one of the lights you will have to turn on if you want to have a great future. *Honouring your parents is one of the master secrets to becoming a distinguished university or college student.*

Fundamentals

❶ Honour means to value, to show care and profound regard.

❷ Honouring your parents will increase your length of days on the earth.

❸ Honouring your parents is the key to your financial future.

Conclusion

Man is born with a need to win, a need to succeed in life. Our minds function from the view of the predator, not the prey. Man craves greatness. We possess an insatiable desire to expand, to grow, and to improve. According to David J. Schwartz in his book titled Maximize Your Mental Power, he says 80 per cent of everything good in life is owned only by 20 per cent of the people? I find this to be an absolute truth. What is the difference between the people who succeed and the people who don't? I submit to you that people are not the same. The differences in people are:

❶ What they are willing to pursue.
❷ Who they have decided to believe.

❸ What gifts or abilities they have decided to strengthen.

❹ What future they are willing to be trained for.

These are just a few of the many other things that distinguish one person from another. The future you are willing to be trained for will distinguish you from others. That will be your point of difference. You must celebrate and magnify your difference; your success is hidden in your uniqueness. I want you to know that you can have a successful future. A life of distinction is waiting for you. Go ahead and climb the ladder of distinction. The ladder does not care who climbs it, and it is not crowded at the top. Decide from this day to live a distinguished life. The day you make a decision about your life is the day your world will change.

Personal Notes

Personal Notes

Personal Notes

Personal Notes

Personal Notes

Personal Notes

Personal Notes

If you desire to contact Bheki Shabangu for life coaching you can visit: **www.successmentorship. co.uk** or

email:info@successmentorship.co.uk.

References

❶ Dr Mike Murdock, *Unstoppable Passion* (Denton Texas: Wisdom Center Publication, 2007).

❷ Andy Stanley, *Visioneering* (Oregon: Multnomah Publishers, 2005).

❸ Dr David Molapo, *If You Are Not Growing, You Are Dying* (South Africa: I CAN Publication, 2001).

❹ Jehiah Czebotar, "Personality Traits". http://www.oneishy.com/personality.

❺ BSM Consulting, "Personality Types". http://www.personalitypage.com.

Appendix 1:

7 Golden Questions

🔒 What do you want to be known for on this earth? How do you want to be remembered?

🔒 Will quitting the pursuit of your dreams bring you joy and satisfaction? If not, what is the price for quitting?

🔒 If you were sitting on the throne as a king or a queen and you noticed a ten pound note blowing in the wind, would you leave the throne to chase the ten pound note?

🔒 Does your life revolve around the opinions of others? If yes, when will you become yourself?

🔒 If everybody were paid the same salary, what would you do for a living?

🔒 If you were blind, what kind of a person would you marry?

🔒 If you had only one year to live, what would you do for your parents?

Appendix 2:

Personality Type

How to work out your personality type? For each question, circle the number that best describes you. (Please circle only one answer per question). On completion, add up your scores to find your temperament.

Question	Score (number circled)
A	
B	
C	
D	
E	
F	

G	
H	
I	
J	
K	
L	
M	
N	
O	
P	
Q	
R	
S	
T	
TOTAL	

Temperament Quiz

(Please circle the number of the answer that describes you best.)

A. **Emotions**: How would you describe your emotional state when dealing with difficult situations?
- ❶ You wear your heart on your sleeve.
- ❷ You turn a cold shoulder to hurtful situations.
- ❸ You are extremely sensitive to hurtful comments.
- ❹ You are calm, controlled, and build your walls up higher.

B. **Emotions**: How do you react in spontaneous stressful situations?
- ❶ Anger wells up, and you let it out.
- ❷ Eyes set on the goal; anyone who can't help you should get out of your way.

❸ You cry and worry about the situation for days afterward.

❹ You put up your defensive wall and go the easiest route.

C. **Logical Thinker or Dreamer**: When you are approached with a problem, how do you find the solution?

❶ You think of innovative ideas and are passionate about them.

❷ You think about the end result and find the most logical route.

❸ You come up with innovative ideas based on detailed analysis.

❹ You don't want to be approached, but can slowly calculate a logical solution.

D. **Logical Thinker or Dreamer**: How would your friends describe you?

❶ Highly imaginative; storyteller.

❷ Practical; dynamic thinker.

❸ Artistic or musical; detail conscious.

❹ Detached observer; diplomatic.

E. **Anger**: What below makes you angriest?

❶ Someone disregards something you are passionate about.

❷ Someone checks your integrity or second guesses you.

❸ Someone says or does something that you think is meant to hurt you.

❹ Not too much of anything. It doesn't matter anyway.

F. **Sensitivity**: When you meet other people, how much do you sense what is going on with them?

❶ Very responsive to others' emotions. You want to cheer them up.

❷ Unfeeling; you hardly sense anything of what they're feeling.

❸ You are highly sensitive to personal anguish, but other emotions aren't felt as much.

❹ You are observant and sense a wide variety of what they feel, but are not limited to just emotional analysis.

G. **Reaction to Change**: When something occurs in your life that requires change, how do you react to it?

❶ Embrace it; change is good.

❷ Adjust, change, and move on; the big picture hasn't changed, only small details.

❸ Analyze the situations and figure out all the problems the change is going to create.

❹ Ignore the change until the last minute possible, hoping you can avoid it.

H. **Forgiveness**: When people wrong you, how do you react?

❶ Get upset, blow up in anger, then forget about it soon after.

❷ Push the offenders aside in your mind and forget about them; it's a small thing to worry about for more than a few minutes.

❸ Be quite at the moment and mutter under your breath about how you plan to get even.

❹ Shrug your shoulders, throw it off, and not say a word to the offenders except in sarcasm.

I. **Pace of Action**: When you are given a task to accomplish, how do you go about doing it?

❶ Passionate about it in the beginning, but lose focus without encouragement.

❷ Head on, not looking to the left or to the right; self-confident.

❸ Analyzing the small details, going over the problems, and presenting your work's results with great attention to detail.

❹ You need a deadline; you'll procrastinate until the right time, then methodically pull it together with efficient, but not exact, detail.

J. **Social Interaction**: When interacting with other people, friends or otherwise, how do you react?

❶ Outgoing; attention-seeking.

❷ Bold; unemotional.

❸ Cautious; listening to complaints or gossip.

❹ Good listener; avoid conflicts and confrontation.

K. **Whom do you identify with?** Of these four people out of the bible, whom do you identify with most?

❶ Peter, who spoke before he thought and jumped out of the boat to greet his friend who walked on the water.

❷ Paul, who stayed strong and bold even when his testimony was drastically changed by a humbling experience.

❸ Moses, who asked God who he was to set God's people free, said that he was not worthy to do so.

❹ Abraham, who didn't ask questions of a source he knew was good, was even willing to sacrifice his son at God's command.

L. **Friendliness**: How would your friends most likely describe you?

❶ Fun to be around; compassionate.

❷ Independent; a bit distant.

❸ Self-sacrificing; problem solver.

❹ Dependable; mediator, pleasant.

M. **Organization**: When you have many things to keep in mind, how well do you organize it?

❶ Leave it to mental check, don't take notes; organization is a waste of time.

❷ Write out goals step-by-step, and look past small details that don't fit them.

❸ Everything is written down and filed exactly where it needs to go.

❹ Filing and note-taking is necessary, but almost is good enough; other people come before organizing your own ideas.

N. **Stubbornness**: When people approach you with new ideas that you don't totally agree with, how do you react?

❶ Listen and embrace the idea if it will gain their acceptance.

❷ Tell them how you feel; stand firm, not caring how loud you get.

❸ Have a deep, philosophical discussion that lasts for hours.

❹ Listen intently. If the source is a good one, you accept it without a word; if it is a bad source, you cast it away, also without a word.

O. **Optimism vs. Pessimism**: How do you look at your life and the world around you?

❶ The world is your oyster, and it's waiting for you to be the star you were born to be.

❷ You have a purpose and a dream, and no one can stomp on either.

❸ You have many problems, and no one could possibly help you sort them out.

❹ Life goes on no matter what happens. There's nothing to get excited about.

P. **Sports**: How do you feel about participating in sports?

❶ You want to be put in the game. You want to play. You want the ball.

❷ You are an aggressive player, but you give pointers to the other players on your team. You play to win.

❸ You would rather read a book, watch television, or do something creative.

❹ You are content to just watch other people play and stay on the sidelines.

Q. **Movies**: What type of movies do you like?

❶ Fast action or slapstick, something that will keep your attention.

❷ If you have time for movies, you like ones with big ideas about people who had big dreams and made them come true.

❸ Comedy and dramas that make you think about your own circumstances.

❹ It doesn't matter one way or the other. Whatever everyone else says is worth watching sounds interesting.

R. **Friends**: How many friends do you have, and how do you feel about making new ones?

❶ You have a lot of friends. You make new friends almost every day.

❷ You don't need many friends, but you like to hang out with positive-minded people.

❸ You have only a couple of close friends, whom you trust. It's hard for you to trust a lot of people. It's a slow process.

❹ You are a loner, but if someone wants to be your friend, you will be there for them no matter what.

S. **Academics**: What subjects in school do/did you like most, and which subjects could you have done without?

❶ Physical education and art kept your attention, for the most part; you got bored with math. English wasn't bad, if the subject matter suited your taste.

❷ Politics and science were fascinating, as long as there wasn't too much math involved. Classes you needed to graduate suited you just fine. You had to make yourself like them.

❸ You didn't have a particular favorite subject. You loved to learn, and the more abstract, the better. Bring on the math class, too. You loved manipulating numbers.

❹ Sociology, psychology, history, and English fascinated you because you liked to understand people and how they interact. You weren't very thrilled about math classes, but if you had to go, oh well.

T. **Writing**: What kind of writing do you like to do?

❶ Simple poetry, prose, and short stories.

❷ You write whatever will get your point across to the reader in whatever form it needs to be.

❸ Abstract poetry with intricate rhythms and flow, such as sonnets. You like to write longer works, such as novels. Essays are also fun to write.

❹ You are content to write whatever suites you at the time. If you are blocked in one type of writing, you'll switch, then go back. You go the route your muse takes you.

Add all the points together to get your final score. Once you've got your final score, use the scoring guide below:

- Total score 20 to 35 – **SANGUINE**
- Total score 36 to 51 – **CHOLERIC**
- Total score 52 to 67 – **MELANCHOLY**
- Total score 68 to 80 – **PHLEGMATIC**

Details of the Personalities

Sanguine

Brief Description of a Sanguine

Sanguines are enthusiastic, idealistic, and creative. They are able to do almost anything that interests them. They have great people skills. They need to live life in accordance with their inner values. They are excited by new ideas, but bored with details. They are open-minded and flexible, with a broad range of interests and abilities.

Strengths of a Sanguine

The Extrovert | The Talker | The Optimist

The Sanguine's Characteristics

- Appealing personality
- Talkative, storyteller
- Life of the party
- Good sense of humour
- Memory for colour
- Physically holds on to listener

- Emotional and demonstrative
- Enthusiastic and expressive
- Cheerful and bubbling over
- Curious
- Good on stage
- Wide-eyed and innocent
- Lives in the present
- Changeable disposition
- Sincere at heart
- Always a child

The Sanguine as a Parent

- Makes home fun
- Is liked by children's friends
- Turns disaster into humour
- Is the circus master

The Sanguine at Work

- Volunteers for jobs
- Thinks up new activities
- Looks great on the surface
- Creative and colourful
- Has energy and enthusiasm
- Starts in a flashy way

- Inspires others to join
- Charms others to work

The Sanguine as a Friend

- Makes friends easily
- Loves people
- Thrives on compliments
- Seems exciting
- Envied by others
- Doesn't hold grudges
- Apologizes quickly
- Prevents dull moments
- Likes spontaneous activities

Weaknesses of a Sanguine

The Extrovert | The Talker | The Optimist

The Sanguine's Characteristics

- Compulsive talker
- Exaggerates and elaborates
- Dwells on trivia
- Can't remember names
- Scares others off
- Too happy for some
- Has restless energy

- Egotistical
- Blusters and complains
- Naive, gets taken in
- Has loud voice and laugh
- Controlled by circumstances
- Gets angry easily
- Seems phoney to some
- Never grows up

The Sanguine as a Parent

- Keeps home in a frenzy
- Forgets children's appointments
- Disorganized
- Doesn't listen to the whole story

The Sanguine at Work

- Would rather talk
- Forgets obligations
- Doesn't follow through
- Confidence fades fast
- Undisciplined
- Priorities out of order
- Decides by feelings
- Easily distracted

- Wastes time talking

The Sanguine as a Friend

- Hates to be alone
- Needs to be centre stage
- Wants to be popular
- Looks for credit
- Dominates conversations
- Interrupts and doesn't listen
- Answers for others
- Fickle and forgetful
- Makes excuses
- Repeats stories

Possible careers for a Sanguine

- Consultant
- Psychologist
- Entrepreneur
- Actor
- Teacher
- Counsellor
- Politician/diplomat
- Writer/journalist
- Television reporter

- Computer programmer/systems analyst/computer specialist
- Scientist
- Engineer

Choleric

Brief Description of a Choleric

Cholerics are friendly, adaptable, and action-oriented. They are "doers" who are focused on immediate results. Living in the here-and-now, they're risk-takers with fast-paced lives. They can be impatient with long explanations. They are extremely loyal to their peers, but not usually respectful of laws and rules if they get in the way of getting things done. They have great people skills.

Strengths of a Choleric

The Extrovert | The Doer | The Optimist

The Choleric's Characteristics

- Born leader
- Dynamic and active
- Compulsive need for change
- Must correct wrongs
- Strong-willed and decisive
- Unemotional
- Not easily discouraged
- Independent and self-sufficient
- Exudes confidence
- Can run anything

The Choleric as a Parent

- Exerts sound leadership
- Establishes goals
- Motivates family to action
- Knows the right answer
- Organizes household

The Choleric at Work

- Goal-oriented
- Sees the whole picture
- Organizes well
- Seeks practical solutions
- Moves quickly to action
- Delegates work
- Insists on production
- Makes the goal
- Stimulates activity
- Thrives on opposition

The Choleric as a Friend

- Has little need for friends
- Will work for group activity
- Will lead and organize
- Is usually right

- Excels in emergencies

Weaknesses of a Choleric

The Extrovert | The Doer | The Optimist

The Choleric's Characteristics

- Bossy
- Impatient
- Quick-tempered
- Can't relax
- Too impetuous
- Enjoys controversy and arguments
- Won't give up when losing
- Comes on too strong
- Inflexible
- Is not complimentary
- Dislikes tears and emotions
- Is unsympathetic

The Choleric as a Parent

- Tends to dominate
- Too busy for family
- Gives answers too quickly
- Impatient with poor performance
- Won't let children relax

- May send them into depression

The Choleric at Work
- Little tolerance for mistakes
- Doesn't analyze details
- Bored by trivia
- May make rash decisions
- May be rude or tactless
- Manipulates people
- Demanding of others
- End justifies the means
- Work may become a god
- Demands loyalty in the ranks

The Choleric as a Friend
- Tends to use people
- Dominates others
- Knows everything
- Decides for others
- Can do everything better
- Is too independent
- Possessive of friends and mate
- Can't say, "I'm sorry"
- May be right, but unpopular

Possible careers for a Choleric

- Sales representatives
- Marketing personnel
- Police/detective work
- Paramedic/emergency medical technician
- PC technicians/network cablers
- Computer technical support
- Entrepreneurs

Melancholy

Brief Description of a Melancholy

Melancholies are logical, original, creative thinkers. They can become very excited about theories and ideas. They are exceptionally capable and driven to turn theories into real-life applications. They highly value knowledge, competence, and logic. Quiet and reserved, they can be hard to get to know well. They are individualistic, having no interest in leading or following others.

Strengths of a Melancholy

The Introvert | The Thinker | The Pessimist

The Melancholy's Characteristics

- Analytical
- Deep and thoughtfully
- Serious and purposeful
- Genius prone
- Talented and creative
- Artistic or musical
- Philosophical and poetic
- Appreciative of beauty
- Sensitive to others
- Self-sacrificing

- Conscientious
- Idealistic

The Melancholy as a Parent

- Sets high standards
- Wants everything done right
- Keeps home in good order
- Picks up after children
- Sacrifices own will for others
- Encourages scholarship and talent

The Melancholy at Work

- Schedule-oriented
- Perfectionist, high standards
- Detail conscious
- Persistent and thorough
- Orderly and organized
- Neat and tidy
- Economical
- Sees the problems
- Finds creative solutions
- Needs to finish what is started
- Likes charts, graphs, figures, lists

The Melancholy as a Friend

- Makes friends cautiously
- Content to stay in background
- Avoids causing attention
- Faithful and devoted
- Will listen to complaints
- Can solve others' problems
- Deep concern for other people
- Moved to tears with compassion
- Seeks ideal mate

Weaknesses of a Melancholy

The Introvert | The Thinker | The Pessimist

The Melancholy's Characteristics

- Remembers the negatives
- Moody and depressed
- Enjoys being hurt
- Has false humility
- Off in another world
- Low self-image
- Has selective hearing
- Self-centred
- Too introspective
- Guilt feelings

- Persecution complex
- Tends to hypochondria

The Melancholy as a Parent

- Puts goals beyond reach
- May discourage children
- May be too meticulous
- Becomes martyr
- Sulks over disagreements
- Puts guilt upon children

The Melancholy at Work

- Not people-oriented
- Depressed over imperfections
- Chooses difficult work
- Hesitant to start projects
- Spends too much time planning
- Prefers analysis to work
- Self-deprecating
- Hard to please
- Standards often too high
- Deep need for approval

The Melancholy as a Friend

- Lives through others
- Insecure socially
- Withdrawn and remote
- Critical of others
- Holds back affections
- Dislikes those in opposition
- Suspicious of people
- Antagonistic and vengeful
- Unforgiving
- Full of contradictions
- Sceptical of compliments

Possible careers for a Melancholy

- Scientists — especially physics, chemistry
- Photographers
- Strategic planners
- Mathematicians
- University professors
- Computer programmers/systems analysts/computer animation/computer specialists
- Technical writers
- Engineers
- Lawyers/attorneys

- Judges
- Forensic scientists
- Forestry specialist/park rangers

Phlegmatic

Brief Description of a Phlegmatic

Phlegmatics are quiet, kind, and conscientious. They can be depended on to follow through. They usually put the needs of others above their own needs. Stable and practical, they value security and traditions. They have a well-developed sense of space and function and a rich inner world of observations about people. They are extremely perceptive of other's feelings and are interested in serving others.

Strengths of a Phlegmatic

The Introvert | The Watcher | The Pessimist

The Phlegmatic's Characteristics

- Low-key personality
- Easygoing and relaxed
- Calm, cool, and collected
- Patient, well-balanced
- Consistent life
- Quiet but witty
- Sympathetic and kind
- Keeps emotions hidden
- Happily reconciled to life
- All-purpose person

The Phlegmatic as a Parent

- Makes a good parent
- Takes time for the children
- Is not in a hurry
- Can take the good with the bad
- Doesn't get upset easily

The Phlegmatic at Work

- Competent and steady
- Peaceful and agreeable
- Has administrative ability
- Mediates problems
- Avoids conflicts
- Good under pressure
- Finds the easy way

The Phlegmatic as a Friend

- Easy to get along with
- Pleasant and enjoyable
- Inoffensive
- Good listener
- Dry sense of humour
- Enjoys watching people
- Has many friends

- Has compassion and concern

Weaknesses of a Phlegmatic

The Introvert | The Watcher | The Pessimist

The Phlegmatic's Characteristics
- Unenthusiastic
- Fearful and worried
- Indecisive
- Avoids responsibility
- Quiet will of iron
- Selfish
- Too shy and reticent
- Self-righteous

The Phlegmatic as a Parent
- Lax on discipline
- Doesn't organize home
- Takes life too easy

The Phlegmatic at Work
- Not goal-oriented
- Lacks self-motivation
- Hard to get moving
- Resents being pushed

- Lazy and careless
- Discourages others
- Would rather watch

The Phlegmatic as a Friend
- Dampens enthusiasm
- Stays uninvolved
- Is not exciting
- Indifferent to plans
- Judges others
- Sarcastic and teasing
- Resists change

Possible careers for a Phlegmatic
- Interior decorators
- Designers
- Nurses
- Administrators/managers
- Administrative/assistants
- Child care/early childhood development
- Social work/counsellors
- Paralegals
- Clergy/religious workers
- Office managers

- Shopkeepers
- Bookkeepers
- Home economics

CPSIA information can be obtained at www.ICGtesting.com
Printed in the USA
BVOW07s0958090215

386954BV00001B/5/P

9 781438 936444